IT'S A CRAZY WORLD...
LEARN FROM IT

Part I: Taking Care of Me

S. L. Young

Dedication:

To my mom, I love you very much. Based on your choices, I am alive and have become the man I am today. For this, I love you beyond any description that can be offered by words.

To my students that challenge me to do more, be better, and expect more.

Life creates opportunities for joy and periods of sadness, and times that our existence is questioned and challenged.

The ability to learn from life experiences, to push past preconceived boundaries, and to help others is part of life's purpose.

Don't spend too much time wondering about past unfulfilled possibilities because the answers are unlikely to be found.

Understand that "It's a Crazy World...Learn from It".

QUEST OF KNOWLEDGE

Knowledge is an adventure and cannot be found in your comfort zone. Don't ever stop learning or searching for the quest of knowledge. The future is coming whether you like it or not...so drive yourself toward a personal pursuit of continuous improvement.

EXPERIENCE VERSUS WISDOM

Experience is a great teacher; however, others' wisdom is a great ally.

RELEASING DEMONS

Retaining past pains will not help to release the chains; however, dealing with the pain will help to release the chains.

EXCUSES STINK

Excuses are like trash, they stink and you don't want to deal with anyone else's.

STARTING POINT FOR EXCUSES

If there's a need to provide an excuse, start with the parts that are the most important ... accountability and ownership.

OPINIONS

Opinions offered in the dark without a face may have questionable value; however, the opinions that mean the most are those that are given in the light by someone that will stand by the opinion.

WEIGHT OF WORDS

Actions can sometimes be misunderstood; however, words are thoughts formulated and communicate an individual's intent.

VALUE OF CRITIQUES

Critics and criticism can be valuable tools for self-improvement, even if the comments are not delivered in the most positive way.

VIEWPOINTS

Unshared viewpoints are similar to hidden gems in that the potential value cannot be fully assessed or appreciated until it's fully exposed.

PRESSURE RELIEF

Options are over for a balloon that was under so much pressure that it popped; recovery begins by releasing pressure long before the maximum capacity is topped.

SERENITY PERSPECTIVE

I'm o.k., you're o.k., and we can both be o.k. even if I don't like your way.

CHALLENGING MOMENTS

Challenging moments in life help to define each of us; the choices made during these times often reflect an individual's true nature.

LIFE VALUE

A life is not a failure. By being born, you're already a success and one has not failed until death…and even that's questionable.

MOVING PAST FAILURE

Failure isn't a final destination; however, failure is an inescapable activity that leads to increased knowledge and growth.

ROADMAP TO SUCCESS…

- Dream (of possibilities)

- Desire (to do more)

- Determination (fueled by belief)

- Drive (to get through the tough times)

- Decisiveness (to make decisions)

- Dedication (to achieve the dream)

DREAMS

Dreams are a critical part of life;
dreams create images of possibilities;
possibilities lead to actions; actions
lead to achieving dreams.

MOVE PASSION FORWARD

Possessing a passion is a gift; however, taking action to support your passion is a skill.

FORGIVENESS

Our past shapes our spirit (the individual within), but our past does not define us. Character is built over a lifetime and not one faulty moment in time ... consider this before shunning someone over a momentary lapse in judgment.

CONFIDENCE

Confidence, not cockiness, can be underrated; therefore, speak with conviction. Individuals may sometimes follow based on the strength of the argument or the conviction of the communication.

CRITICAL ELEMENTS OF COMMUNICATION:

- Clear

- Crisp

- Concise

- Confident

- Connectedness

- Compassionate

- Control

- Conviction

REQUIREMENTS FOR CHANGE

Change requires a decision to take action, ownership, and control.

IMPORTANCE OF COURAGE

Courage is an extraordinary skill that drives action despite any potential negative feedback (internal or external) that would otherwise prevent progress.

LIFE DOESN'T WAIT

Life will not wait for you to get ready; you're the one that needs to catch-up.

LACK OF ACTION

Inaction won't lead to action; however, inaction will lead to significant dissatisfaction.

ATTITUDE

Attitude drives your motivation, change your attitude and the possibilities of success are endless.

ENGAGING IN LIFE REQUIRES…

- Considering Available Options

- Evaluating Choices

- Making a Decision

- Executing a Plan

Evaluating choices without making a decision is a waste of time and making a decision to take action without execution is pointless.

CHOICES

Choices are critical decision points in life. However, individual power begins with the ability to make a decision and take action to implement. Without a choice, a decision, and action individuals are left with unfulfilled dreams.

POWER OF CHOICE

The power of choice is underrated, as there is seldom a time that individuals do not influence their destiny by making or in some cases not making a choice.

VULNERABILITY

Sharing your past, your fears, and your dreams presents opportunities to connect in much deeper ways that create genuine connections.

RESILIENCE

The ability to recover from past challenges and move forward is the difference between those that watch things happen and those that make things happen.

CONTINUE TO GO

Others' noes shouldn't mean that you shouldn't continue to go.

SEIZING OPPORTUNITY

An opportunity can sometimes seem to appear out of nowhere; don't question it, capture it.

OPPORTUNITY AND ENVIRONMENT

Given the opportunity and a supportive environment, most of us will adjust to achieve success. However, in the absence of a supportive environment, personal drive is an individual's best friend.

INDIVIDUAL MOTIVATION

Motivation is very personal, unique to each of us. No one can motivate you, but you. However, others can help to identify those things that will cause individuals to develop their own motivation.

PROBABILITY OF SUCCESS

The probability of success is zero if the first step towards a goal is not taken; however, the probability of future success increases exponentially with each subsequent step.

DEALING WITH NEGATIVE INDIVIDUALS

Sometimes getting negative individuals involved with making decisions and leading activities can minimize their desire to complain since it's their work that would be at the nature of the complaint.

However, 'truly' negative individuals will always find something to complain about perhaps to make themselves feel more important.

INTERNAL STRENGTH

Individual strength is derived from continuing to move forward despite negative things that might have happened.

WASTED TIME

Too much time is spent worrying about opinions that don't matter instead of spending 100% of time considering the most important opinion ... yours.

STAY THE COURSE

The things others say don't matter if you know the things are not true. Individuals should continue to be themselves and do things that are helpful, as individuals will sometimes say things just to hurt someone or to make themselves feel better.

A DIFFERENT VIEW

Just because an individual has low expectations for themselves doesn't mean that others should sanction them.

EXPECTATIONS

Expectations are the starting point for great performance. If expectations are low, then the effort provided may reach the same level; therefore, don't discount anyone's options. Require more and set high expectations for yourself and others.

CLARITY OF PURPOSE

Each of us has perspectives, some right and some wrong; however, the ability to distinguish the truth begins with the capability to process input and transform the input into information that is useful; otherwise, the input is just noise.

INTERNAL CONFLICT

At times, while making a decision, there will be conflict between the thoughts in your head and the emotions in your heart. In these times, and others, it's often useful to trust your gut, which is an internal barometer of one's thoughts.

DECISION MAKING GUIDELINES

- Think with your brain;

- Listen to your heart;

- Trust your gut.

MANAGE YOUR COMPASS

Don't let another individual's limitations be the compass for your success. Success is not a destination, and your pursuits will never be achieved if the compass used has artificial limitations.

CONTROL RESPONSE

You can't control the things that individuals do to you; however, you can control your response to the things that happen to you.

CONTROL BOUNDARIES

You can only control those things that are within your power, anything else is out of your control or potentially none of your business.

This does not mean to stop fighting for positive change.

FUELED BY FEAR

Fear can compel you to action or cause you to be stifled from achieving personal greatness.

<u>FEARS ARE OPPORTUNITIES -</u>
<u>CONQUERING FEARS REQUIRES:</u>

- Patience

- Passion

- Planning

- Persistence

- Perseverance

- Pain

- Perspective

- Purpose

- Positivity

MOVING PAST FEARS

Choice, and not fear, is generally the reason for a lack of progress; getting past fears requires a choice, a decision, and the willingness to take a chance.

FEAR'S SOURCE

Fear does not always hold you back; individual inaction is usually the real culprit.

FEAR MANTRA

- No fears…

- No doubts…

- No worries…

MANAGING FEAR

Fear is something that can hold you back or propel you to greatness.

PERSONAL COURAGE

The ability to move past your fears despite personal or societal reservations is 'real' courage.

LIFE AND BUSINESS ARE ABOUT...

- Character

- Honesty

- Humility

- Attitude (Positive)

- Respect for Others

- Intelligence (Emotional and Mental)

- Self-Respect

- Morals

- Acceptance of Others and their Views

DIRTY SUCCESS

If you need to step on someone to win, then you must really question the individual within.

PERSONAL COMPROMISE

A compromise on ethical or moral philosophies is a slippery slope; once the slide down the slope has started, it's very difficult to go back up.

VALUE OF MONEY

It's better to be broke and in love with yourself, than rich and not know yourself.

MONEY PERSPECTIVE

Money does not define the individual within; money only helps to provide the material things that are obtained; self-worth is priceless and cannot and should not be bought by material compensation.

MEASURE OF SUCCESS

Material success is measured by tangible items; real (impacting and lasting) success is measured by the individuals helped by your success.

RESPONSIBLE POWER

Power may be derived from the rights granted, but 'responsible' power considers the impact (positive or negative) of the power on others.

TAKING YOURSELF SERIOUSLY

Don't take yourself too seriously. There are many things that require a serious focus; however, a perception of a serious issue may only be a trivial concern in the grand scheme of life.

SELF-WORTH

Self-worth is not based on the way others see me or want me to be; instead, it's based on my perception of me.

DIGNITY AND SELF-RESPECT

After taking away all of your material possessions, there are only two (2) things that remain: dignity and self-respect. Don't relinquish these to anyone, ever.

CHARACTER TEST

It's very easy to have character if others are watching; however, true character is defined by the things an individual does while no one is watching. That's the best test of character.

STRENGTH AND COURAGE

The strength to stand-alone to forge new ground even if others do not share your views is extreme courage; doing something positive, the thing you know is correct in your heart, even if others do not agree is an immeasurable strength.

FUTURE SUCCESS

Your future and your success are directly correlated to the energy, focus, and commitment applied to achieving your goal.

SUCCESS

Success is directly correlated to the actions taken today and the adjustments made along the way.

SECRET INGREDIENTS OF SUCCESS

The secret ingredients of success start with accountability and determination.

PASSION FOR SUCCESS

Passion is an important element of success; without passion, the effort can be mediocre. Passion provides the fuel that maintains the fire to persevere while the possibility of success is limited.

RECOGNIZE OTHERS

Listen to and often recognize individuals, as these are the contributions that matter.

SHARED ACCOMPLISHMENTS

No matter the things accomplished in life or the things that will be accomplished, someone else helped.

TRUE FRIENDS

Friends will often come and go; however, true friends will always show, because they're the ones that help us grow.

HOPE

Hope is useful for action, to do more, and to be better; without hope, each task can be much heavier.

PERSPECTIVE

- The past – Is over

- The present – Is now

- The future – Hasn't happened

- There's nothing that can be done to change the past

- The present is within one's control

- Creating and executing a plan (now) will effect one's future

Move forward each day knowing that others have faced similar challenges.

Learning and benefiting from dynamic experiences is part of life's joy.

Continue to dream and work on the opportunities in front of and not behind you.

Understand that "It's a Crazy World…Learn from It".

Made in the USA
Charleston, SC
09 November 2013